MW00889337

Name

Address